Girl Truths

Andrea Carey

CUMBERLAND HOUSE
NASHVILLE, TENNESSEE

GIRL TRUTHS
PUBLISHED BY CUMBERLAND HOUSE PUBLISHING
431 Harding Industrial Drive
Nashville, Tennessee 37211

ISBN 1-58182-463-7

Cover design: James Duncan, James Duncan Creative
Book design: Mary Sanford

Printed in the United States of America
2 3 4 5 6 7—10 09 08 07 06

Lovingly dedicated to the memory of my mother,

Donna Wilson Bell Perrett,

without whom this book would not have been possible.

A few years ago, I started talking to my mother. To anyone who knows our family, this will sound strange, because if there is one thing our family was never short of, it was conversation. But after she was diagnosed with cancer, we found time to really talk together. For the first time, I was able to appreciate this woman as a person—full of humor, grand schemes, ideas, and laughter. In my life she made the leap from being my mother to also being a great friend. We talked and laughed aloud about everything: childhood, mothering, parenting, men, and girlfriends, and I gained new respect and understanding for the women in my family. I come from a long line of opinionated, outspoken, wonderful women—Southern women who would not hesitate to tell you exactly what they thought about anything, and could deliver even harsh truths while making sure you understood they loved you anyway. I know now that makes me a very lucky person.

After her cancer returned, my mother and I began work on a project for my daughter, Lauren. We started writing down things we had learned, advice we had been given, and bits of wisdom we had picked up from both family and friends as we had traveled through life. Simple truths, easy to remember, mostly common sense, but powerful in their simplicity. We wanted to be able to leave a record—to say, "These are the things we want you to know," even after we were no longer here to say them.

With much input from my mother and my sister (a formidable woman in her own right), this book was created. In writing it I have realized both how lucky I am to have had people in my life to give me advice along the way and also how many girls out there face the challenges and unknowns of growing up without anyone to share life lessons with them. The world is a different place for our daughters than it was for our generation, and it is light-years away from what it was in our mothers' time. Yet some truths still apply, and some experiences are universal.

In December 2002, I lost my mother as my muse, but not the dedication to see this project through to completion. The book you hold is the end result of our efforts to place small signposts along the road of my daughter's life to show her where we had walked before her. I have come to realize there are many girls out there who do not have people in their lives to talk to them when they need to talk, or to simply say, "I understand, I've felt that way before." If this book provides wise words to even one girl who needs to hear them and cannot get them elsewhere, my hopes for it have been fulfilled. This is a gift from my family of "girls" to girls in other families, wherever and whoever they may be.

To the girls who are reading this book: I hope you will find words inside that make you laugh, phrases that make you think, and things that you can relate to. You have a long and winding road ahead of you, full of twists and turns, with unseen joys and dilemmas lurking around every corner. Life is both unpredictable and wonderful. It can make you so gloriously happy you laugh out loud, and can also be so unfair that you want to rage and shake your fist at the sky. Do both, but live fully. Life doesn't begin when you reach a certain goal or a certain age; it is going on around you right now. With the input of many girls your age, I believe I have caught a glimpse of the world you live in today. I stand in wonder at the journey you have ahead of you and in awe of the women you will become.

Girl Truths

The Girls you see
in magazines and on TV
look a lot like you
in real life.

There are huge teams of people working to make them
look good for the cameras.
If you and I had that many people concentrating on us every morning,
we might be able to compare.
But we don't.
Those girls have bad hair days,

and get PIMPLES and CAVITIES just like the rest of us.

SO DON'T BEAT YOURSELF UP.

That kind of perfection doesn't exist in the real world.
Nobody looks like that every day.

Adults should never ask you to keep BIG SECRETS.

You have enough to deal with **without** being asked to shoulder
emotional responsibility for an adult.

Not secrets like where a birthday present is hidden—
MAJOR SECRETS—
ones an adult tells you that you can't tell anyone.

You are under NO obligation to keep to yourself
something you feel is *illegal, immoral, or just plain wrong.*

Secrets like these are

little anchors on your soul,

dragging you down.

Cut them loose by talking about them to someone,
and if it happens again, explain that you

CAN'T AND WON'T

be expected to keep a grown-up's secrets to yourself.

Fear can make people act mean.

They may not look or seem scared—
but a lot of bad behavior springs **solely from fear.**

Maybe they are afraid people will see

they aren't **as cool,**

or **as smart,**

or **as popular** as they seem.

YOU DON'T HAVE TO FIGURE IT OUT.

People and animals will **attack** when they get scared or feel cornered.
They attack anything and anybody that gets close to them.

Understand this and give them—friend or foe—
s p a c e   a n d   t i m e   t o   c o o l   o f f.

The world is a huge place.

Your destiny may lie outside your hometown
or even your home country.

There are places, people, and cultures more different
from ours than you can possibly imagine.

The person you choose to spend your life with
may be growing up on the other side of

the nation, the world,
or just across the street.

YOU JUST DON'T KNOW.

Be prepared and knowledgeable enough to follow your path
wherever it may take you.

Expand your horizons.

Women who came before us
have thrown open doors in
medicine, science, law, and politics.
Take advantage of every opportunity before you.

Be strong.

Be smart.

Be self-assured.

Know you are beautiful.

THERE IS NOTHING THAT CAN STOP YOU.

If anyone DOUBTS your abilities because you are a woman,
that just makes it easier for your talents to
CATCH THEM OFF-GUARD.

A strong and intelligent woman
is a force to be reckoned with.

Real friends LIKE you
just for YOU.

Some people don't know you exist until you have
something they want.

They get it or find something else that interests them . . .
then they leave.

A friend who likes you only when they need something
is NOT a friend.

Find those who love you for who you are.

You have plenty to offer
before you add anything you own.

Where you come from is not important—only where you are GOING.

Where you end up in life is solely up to YOU.

You can go just as easily from
nothing to something
as you can from
everything to nothing.
The circumstances you are living in right now
are the results of decisions that the adults in your life made,
good or bad.
Their decisions can't guarantee your *future success.*

Just as important—

they are not an excuse for you not to try to do better.

Some people will have easier paths to success than you will—
that is just the way life is.

You will rise or fall on your own ability and effort.
IT IS YOUR CHOICE WHERE YOU END UP.

Appreciate diversity and differences.

Being different is what makes people interesting. We have

different hair, eye, and skin colors;
different beliefs and religions.

Avoid stereotypes; after all:

Blondes and athletes are not always dumb
Boys aren't always better at math and science,
Girls can do a whole lot more than take care of other people

Look for similarities, not differences.

See past the surface.

A person's looks can't tell you about who they really are.

You have to get to know them.

You got to this point by taking one step at a time.

Stay in motion.
Focus on your future.
Learn to not cling to the past.

While you are spending time dwelling on your past,
your present is becoming it.

Recognize triumphs and mistakes and then go on to the
next challenge.

LOOK AHEAD.

You will get no farther
if you obsess too long about

where you are right now
or where you've been.

You are creating your own history
and working toward your future.

Appreciate simple joys.

What makes you really happy?

Hot cider in the autumn?

Laughing until your stomach hurts?

Jumping into really cold water on a hot summer day?

The smell of little puppies and babies?

Trees that are perfect for climbing?

None of this is **EARTH-SHATTERING STUFF,**
and none of these things cost anything.

BUT THEY ARE IMPORTANT,
because it's the little things that make our lives so very wonderful.

*And life is wonderful,
never forget that.*

The things that make you happy are
as individual as you are.

When life starts getting you down, seek them out,
and take a moment to simply be happy, because

a life not truly enjoyed

is a life not fully lived.

Be proud
to be smart.

Don't ever get caught up in

"playing dumb"

to impress a boy
or fit in.

Smart women are beautiful,
and beautiful women should ALWAYS be smart.

Good looks alone get dull **really fast.**

Unfortunately, this applies to us
as well as potential boyfriend material out there!

When you feel

INSECURE

OR UNDER ATTACK

your first reaction may be to take it out on somebody else.

This doesn't fix the real problem:
whatever is making you miserable.

*Making somebody feel rotten
won't make you feel any better.*

Life is not a competition.

It doesn't make you a bigger or better person to take down those around you.

All that does is prove that your priorities are messed up.

Hurting others makes you a very small person.

You deserve the best—
refuse to accept less.

Set your standards high.

You DESERVE:

fabulous friends,

wonderful opportunities,

and nice things

AS MUCH AS ANYBODY ELSE.

That doesn't mean they will come to you quickly or easily.

You may have to work very hard to get what you want.
You may have to do without while you save for something nice.

But when you get what you really wanted all along—

it will be worth it!

WATCH YOUR LANGUAGE.

Let's face it, by now
you have probably heard most of the "BAD" words
and could use them if you wanted to.

But why?

If what you are saying is important enough to be heard,
use language that will make people receptive to it
instead of words that make you sound
unimaginative and uneducated.

If you can't see any way to say something
without *littering* your language with verbal debris,
you either need to expand your vocabulary
or let the point go.

Keep a journal.

Everything is so vivid in your life right now,
you think you will never forget how you are feeling.
But as you get older your memories will be filtered
through your adult experiences and emotions,
which changes *everything*.

You need to record the history of YOU.

Create it for no one but you.
Find a way to be free to put down
what you really think and feel
without the fear that somebody else will JUDGE you for it.

As you leave behind each stage of life, remember,
the person you were then will never exist again.

There will never be anyone who
**looks just like you, thinks about life as you do,
or dreams the dreams you have.**

Record YOUR reality.

Believe in yourself.

You have **everything** you need to succeed **right now.**
People may try to make you **doubt** yourself,
but **don't let them.**

All of life's possibilities are yours.

Let negative input serve as **fuel** for you
to **prove** you can do
whatever you set your mind to.

Many of the most well-known people in the world
succeeded—despite the fact that
they were **the only ones** who believed
in their ideas or themselves.
Don't give up before you get started.

Many times SUCCESS simply comes
down to SELF-CONFIDENCE.

Be clean.

It doesn't matter **how much money** you have
or what **type of clothes** you wear.

If your hair, clothes, or body are DIRTY,
you are sending the message that

YOU AREN'T WORTH THE EFFORT

and that's how people will treat you.

Even if you are the MOST BEAUTIFUL GIRL in the world—

if you SMELL ODD or LOOK DIRTY,
that is how you will be remembered.

That's not how you want people to remember you.

Being mean and hurtful to people
is something that will HAUNT you.

Even if someone deserves it, doing or saying **hateful things**
is not something you will remember happily.

How do I know?

I still remember **hurtful things** I did
and *never* had the opportunity to apologize for.

AND I REGRET EVERY ONE OF THEM.

I should have been able to LAUGH or JUST WALK AWAY.

Even when I got some satisfaction from a **quick, nasty comeback,**
I don't look back at those times proudly.

AND YOU WON'T EITHER.

Develop your own look.

Developing **your own look** doesn't mean

spending lots of money
or looking like everyone else.

It *DOES* mean you find

what is comfortable—
what looks really good on you—
a look that defines who you are.

Remember, what works for
your mother or your friends
may not be right for you.

Just have FUN and experiment!

Cigarettes will make your teeth YELLOW
and your hair and clothes STINK.

How much would you be willing to pay
someone to **ruin your looks** and **kill you?**

There are millions of people out there
spending a fortune
to buy cigarettes every day.

If you smoke,
you will smell bad,
your teeth will turn yellow,
and sooner or later it will make you very, very sick.

THERE IS NOTHING SEXY OR GROWN-UP ABOUT THAT.

Besides, there are much more fun things
to spend your money on.

Raise your hand.

Give the answer.

Volunteer.

Laugh out loud.

There is NOTHING WRONG
with living your life in a way that shows you are not afraid
to ENJOY YOURSELF, and shows off WHAT YOU CAN DO.

I missed out on a lot of great people and opportunities—
NOT BECAUSE PEOPLE DIDN'T LIKE ME,
but because they didn't notice I was there.

I know it seems easier
to keep quiet and stay in the background—
but you've got **too much going for you** to try to be invisible.

DON'T BE AFRAID TO LEAVE YOUR MARK OR MAKE AN IMPRESSION.

Don't be afraid to be noticed.

*You won't make friends
by pretending to be someone
you are not.*

You may be able to pretend
to be somebody you are not,
but where does that *really* get you?

What happens when your friends find out
that you're somebody **completely different?**

What happens when the real "you"
needs somebody to talk to?

**WHERE DO YOU TURN
IF NONE OF YOUR FRIENDS REALLY KNOW YOU?**

*The world of "make-believe" in friendship
is a **very lonely** place.*

Food is nothing more than **FUEL.**

Depriving your body of food to prove
how much control you have is self-defeating.

*If you go without food long enough,
you will be forced to be completely dependent
on someone to save you from yourself.*

You will have **NO CONTROL OVER YOUR LIFE** until you are well.

At the other extreme,
food cannot make problems GO AWAY
or make you FEEL BETTER ABOUT yourself emotionally.

You can eat huge amounts every time you are blue or bored,
but that cannot make you happy. All it will do
is make you sluggish, heavy, and regretful.

Enjoy in moderation.

If you are blue, bored, or feeling out of control—
call a friend, take a walk, or do some other type of physical activity.

Don't let food become a CRUTCH OR an ENEMY—
it is neither.

Dream big dreams, have big ideas.

Don't limit yourself.

There are so many big things in our world
that need fixing or someone to make them better.

There is no reason that YOU can't be the one to do it.

All that is required is for someone to go
beyond the dreaming stage and **make it happen.**

Just figure out where there is a *need,* or something that
needs *improvement,* then work toward making
YOUR SOLUTION A REALITY.

Who knows—you may change history!

Some people can make you feel bad about yourself.
Just being around them can wear you out.
All the fun gets drained away and
they start sucking you into their misery.

guilt,
constant blame,
or just bad attitude
are real friendship killers—for good reason.

Don't spend your time around people
who make you feel BAD.

YOU DESERVE BETTER.

Find people who appreciate you.

Escape toxic relationships.

Not everyone is going to like you.

We all want to be universally liked,
but sometimes people just don't get along.

One woman I know just doesn't like me.
I haven't really done anything.

I JUST BUG HER,
for no apparent reason.

AND . . .

THAT'S OK.

That doesn't mean we aren't nice to each other.
We just recognize we will never be best buddies.

IF THIS HAPPENS TO YOU, DON'T WORRY ABOUT IT.

It doesn't mean there is anything wrong with either of you.

Be approachable.

Such a simple shortcut to popularity.
So much **easier** than figuring out the

"IN" look, crowd, or attitude.

Just make yourself someone
others are comfortable being around.

Make eye contact;
smile;
say "Hi";
listen to what they say.

Sounds too easy, doesn't it?

BUT IT REALLY WORKS.

You won't believe how many people you will get to know.

Nothing lasts forever.

It is so important to put life into perspective.
Even if it seems like something is going to
make you miserable forever,

IT WON'T.

Forever is a LONG time.

All the time you've lived is only a tiny portion of your life.

A friend committed suicide many years ago. His life just became too
much for him to take. I MISS HIM STILL. I wish I'd had the chance to
stop him or just to tell him to wait it out.

EVERYTHING CHANGES.
EVEN THE MOST IMPOSSIBLE SITUATIONS GET BETTER WITH TIME.

Please, don't ever let yourself despair enough to seek
such a horribly permanent solution to a temporary problem.
Even if you think that no one will notice if you are gone—

THEY WILL.

A life cut short is an impossibly cruel thing
for people left behind to deal with.

There are bad people.
There are good people.

Learn to tell
the difference.

Others will not always have **your best interests** at heart.
There are some people who seem to make everyone miserable.

Some are MEAN on purpose. Some are just SO SELF-ABSORBED they
don't notice or don't care when they hurt someone's feelings.

You don't have to know WHY they are that way,
or even **try to change them.**

Just limit the time you spend with them, if any.

EVERYTHING you want to learn about is in a book.

And all that knowledge **doesn't cost anything.**

Not a cent.

Just go to any library and start looking around
for things that catch your eye.

Read as much as you can.

There is information about **almost everything,**
but if there is something specific
you are interested in that isn't available—
think about writing the book yourself.

Somebody's going to do it—why not YOU?

Earn the things you want.

IF YOU WANT:

a nice house,

to travel,

to be wealthy,

EARN IT.

IF YOU WANT:

to have lots of friends,

to be the class president,

or to be the president of the United States,

YOU *CAN* DO IT.

But there aren't any shortcuts in real life.

Start small and
give yourself enough time to reach your goals.

Anything worth having must be earned.

Have you ever woken up in the morning and felt like **SNARLING** at everybody—a day when even YOUR CAT makes you mad?

Sure you have.

We all have REALLY ROTTEN DAYS,
and many times there is no real reason.
Let the people you care about know up front that

YOU WANT TO BE LEFT ALONE.

Sometimes they will stay away; sometimes they won't—
but at least they've been warned.
AND TOMORROW IS ANOTHER DAY.
You may have to apologize a few times, but you'll get through it.

But remember, after making everybody deal with
YOU AND YOUR BAD DAY,

You may have to deal with THEIRS!

Everyone has the right to have a
bad day once in a while.

You, and only you,
are responsible for your own happiness.

You can get **ANGRY** with
your parents, your friends, or your circumstances,
but the fact is that

NOTHING

outside of yourself can make you happy.

PEOPLE HAVE TRIED TO FIND HAPPINESS THROUGH

position,
money,
power,
and fame,

BUT IT JUST DOESN'T LAST.

Happiness can be found only in

who we are—not in things we have or do.

If a person or a situation
feels WRONG or SCARY to you—

GET AWAY, FAST!

*It is better to run the risk of looking foolish
than to end up in danger.*

Your instincts can be **powerful tools**
if you give yourself
the freedom to trust them.

Don't try to figure out WHAT is setting off alarms
while it is happening.

Trust yourself enough to know that there is a reason
and reflect on it AFTER you are in a safer place.

Trust your instincts.

There are **DRUGS** and
SEXUALLY TRANSMITTED DISEASES
that can **RUIN** your life

the f i r s t time

you experiment.

You will encounter this kind of pressure SOONER OR LATER.

KNOW these situations will arise,
and KNOW where you stand

BEFORE IT HAPPENS.

If you don't have an adult to talk to about drugs and/or sex,
find a book that deals with these issues in a straightforward manner.

There is simply too much at stake to trust information
you get only from other kids.

Don't gamble your life on a quick decision.

Have your response prepared.
Know you always have the final say.

If you have any doubts
whether something is right for you,

THE **DOUBT ALONE** IS REASON ENOUGH
TO SAY "NO" VERY FIRMLY AND LEAVE.

Whatever happens, **GOOD OR BAD,**
it all just becomes part of

YOUR STORY.

Your life is a story
all about and starring you.

There are **PLOT TWISTS AND SURPRISING EVENTS**
we can't foresee.
How you react to them is up to you.

Think about your favorite book or show—
the star rarely knows at the time WHY things are happening.

BUT IT ALL WORKS OUT IN THE END.

Everything—**GOOD OR BAD**—is part of YOUR story.
So . . . flip the page, and eagerly move on to the next chapter.

Something EXCITING is bound to happen!

Be willing to help others.

But if you keep getting caught in
a whirlpool
of someone else's constant disasters—

WISH THEM THE BEST AND MOVE ON.

We all want to be
a white knight and
RESCUE the people around us,

BUT PEOPLE HAVE TO SAVE THEMSELVES.

Tough situations sometimes teach truths
you can't learn any other way.

It is NOT YOUR RESPONSIBILITY to save anyone.

Plan ahead and work hard.

There are no
GENIES THAT WILL GRANT YOU WISHES,
and the chances of you discovering that you are
A LONG-LOST PRINCESS OR MILLIONAIRE are pretty slim.

In the real world, it is amazing how much
GOOD LUCK resembles HARD WORK.

Being terribly poor is NO FUN.
It is sometimes hard to avoid, and
always difficult and stressful.

No one plans to have financial difficulties,
but it can happen.

Leaving your career and life
TO FATE
is too chancy to base your whole future on.

Work to tip the scales in your favor.

I used to *sneak* into my dad's closet
when I was little and shine all of his shoes.

I would very carefully put them back exactly where I found them.
Then I wouldn't say anything—I would just wait.

Sooner or later, he would see them all shiny and be *so happy.*

When you do little unexpectedly nice things for people,
even if they never find out it was you,
IT STILL AFFECTS **THEM.**

It makes you FEEL GOOD to know you made
somebody's day BRIGHTER.

GIVE IT A TRY!

Do nice things for people—
without letting anyone know what you've done.

TIME REALLY DOES HEAL MANY WOUNDS.

Bad things are sometimes TOO BIG
for us to deal with right away.

It is like holding a book too close to your eyes.

YOU CAN'T MAKE SENSE OF IT.

Only by moving it a little farther away will it come into FOCUS.

I really miss my mom, but I've been told that
with time, the very things that bring pain:

the smell of her perfume—
daisies—
old photos—
her favorite color—

will become the things that trigger happy memories for me.

I'M NOT THERE YET, BUT I'M WILLING TO GIVE IT TIME.

Kids aren't responsible for
WHERE THEY LIVE OR HOW MUCH MONEY THEY HAVE.

They are living with the outcome,
GOOD OR BAD,
of decisions made by the adults in their lives.

What they have now doesn't have any bearing on
where they are going or what they will do with their lives.

No amount of money can make
a hateful person attractive, and

no amount of blame can
lift someone above what they are willing to work for.

TRAIN YOUR EYES to see the people underneath the trappings—
STUNNING OR SHABBY.

GOOD PEOPLE WILL SHINE NO MATTER WHAT THEIR CIRCUMSTANCES.

Kids can't be judged by what they have.

Avoid giving out unsolicited advice.

NOBODY LIKES A KNOW-IT-ALL.

Unless someone asks for your input, try to just listen instead of talking.

Even if you think you have a great solution, make sure the person is looking for advice.

Most people need you
to simply listen—
and to understand—

not to fix the problem for them.

LIFE IS NOT FAIR.

FRIENDS AND FAMILY LEAVE.
PEOPLE WE LOVE DIE.
THINGS HAPPEN THAT WE DON'T DESERVE.

*Events may knock you completely off balance for a while,
or they may completely change the course you are on.*

Getting angry or staying sullen doesn't help.

**YOU CAN SIT IN A PUDDLE OF SELF-PITY
AND RAGE ABOUT HOW IT'S "NOT FAIR."**

But that doesn't solve the problem.

LIFE IS UNPREDICTABLE, SO GET *creative* . . .
YOU CAN DEAL WITH WHATEVER IT DISHES OUT.

It is OK to feel sad or hurt.

There is NOTHING WRONG with crying when you are sad
or telling someone when they have hurt you.

You don't have to DEFEND YOUR EMOTIONS,
but you do have the responsibility to tell people
how they made you feel.

WHAT THEY DO WITH THE INFORMATION IS UP TO THEM.

Humans are the only animals that cry to express sadness.
And sometimes a good cry helps when nothing else can.

If it gets bad enough, let the tears flow,
preferably when you are alone or with people you trust.

Then dry your eyes, blow your nose,

AND MOVE ON!

Try as many new activities as you can.

You may find out that you are really good at something,
or really enjoy a sport you didn't expect to.

If you really love it,
but you aren't very good when you first start—

keep trying.
And give yourself a break!

Most things just take practice to get right.

The reason talent is SO ADMIRED is because of the
DEDICATION
it takes to be REALLY GOOD.

IF EVERYONE CAN DO SOMETHING WELL WITHOUT EVEN TRYING,
IT ISN'T REALLY THAT IMPRESSIVE, IS IT?

Just have fun when you try something new.

Things that happen are not always about YOU.

There is a lot of stuff that may happen
to you and around you that is

NOT YOUR FAULT.

Your family may be struggling.
Your parents may be divorcing.
Someone you love may leave you.
A friend may make a decision that really messes up their life.

NONE OF THIS KIND OF STUFF
—NO MATTER HOW IT MAY AFFECT YOU—
IS BECAUSE OF YOU.

It takes time to make these situations better.
You have to tough it out—but remember . . .

You may have to deal with the situation,
but there is no way you could have caused it.

Love being
"DIFFERENT."

FIND YOUR OWN LOOK;
BE YOUR OWN PERSON.

It's so much better than trying to look or act like everybody else.

And it's one way to guarantee
PEOPLE WILL REMEMBER YOU!

It makes it so much easier to know who you are,
instead of trying to conform to somebody else's ideal.

You may set an example for someone else to
BREAK OUT OF THE EXPECTED MOLD
and become their own person.

What a great gift to give—just by being true to yourself—
and setting a fearless example!

It's SO EXCITING when you notice someone is paying you
extra attention or you hear somebody **really likes** you.

But what if you really aren't attracted to them?

The **kindest** thing you can do is let them know
you just don't feel the same way.
And let them know **as soon** as you figure it out.

You won't be doing them **any favors** by pretending,
or **trying to make yourself like them** in return.

*Set yourself and them free to look for someone
who is better suited for both of you.*

Think how it would feel if you thought someone **really liked** you,
only to find out they had only been pretending.

OUCH!

You don't have to like
every boy that likes you.

Be adaptable.

CLASSY—

CALM—

COLLECTED—

CENTERED—

CONFIDENT—

COMFORTABLE—

Wherever you are.

THIS IS ADAPTABILITY—

one of the most enviable traits you can embody.

It has absolutely **nothing** to do with
how much money you have or your station in life.

Not changing your personality depending on who you are around,
but being able to be

your own wonderful, unique self—

and **feel at home** in **any** social situation.

When you can do this effortlessly, you will have become

a rare and unforgettable woman.

You never know where life is going to take you.

BE ADAPTABLE ENOUGH TO FOLLOW WHEREVER YOUR PATH MAY LEAD.

Doing NOTHING IS making a decision.

Don't ever think that by ignoring a decision

. . . it goes away.

At times there is NO clear-cut "RIGHT" answer.

These are the trickiest decisions to make.

Imagine a big plate of cookies in front of you:

peanut butter, coconut, and chocolate chip.

If you like them all and
don't really care what kind you get
or if you even get one at all,
THEN JUST SIT BACK AND LET EVERYBODY ELSE GRAB THEM.

But . . . if you really HATE coconut and peanut butter
and will only be happy if you get the chocolate chip,
YOU HAD BETTER REACH OUT AND GRAB ONE.

LIFE IS NOT A PLATE OF COOKIES
(OR A BOWL OF CHERRIES, FOR THAT MATTER!).
IF A CERTAIN OUTCOME IS IMPORTANT TO YOU,
CHOOSE IN A WAY TO MAKE IT HAPPEN.

Don't look back later and try to
BLAME LUCK OR FATE
when things don't go the way you want, if you
refused to commit.

Make your own decisions. Follow your own path.

Think your own thoughts.

Treasure the things that make you different.

AND DON'T WORRY ABOUT WHAT EVERYONE ELSE IS DOING OR THINKING.

There has **never** been anyone **just like you,**
and there is a **reason** you are here.

Things that are impossible to replace or
duplicate are called PRICELESS.

Something being the only one of its kind makes it
impossibly valuable—RARE AND UNIQUE.

I'M TALKING ABOUT YOU.

Celebrate your individuality.

GOSSIP HURTS—

TRUE OR NOT.

HAVE YOU EVER HAD THAT AWFUL FEELING
THAT EVERYBODY IS SAYING SOMETHING ABOUT YOU?

The terrible thing about **gossip** is that it doesn't have to be true to
SPREAD LIKE A WILDFIRE.

It's kind of **exciting**
when somebody wants to tell you a secret about somebody else.

This is the DANGER of gossip—
sometimes stories grow because each person adds
JUST A LITTLE BIT TO MAKE IT MORE INTERESTING
until the story has grown to a **horrible size.**

If you hear a rumor—
DON'T TELL EVEN ONE OTHER PERSON.

**Make it stop with you.
That's all you can do.**

Our world needs more heroes.

BE ONE.

YOU DON'T HAVE TO WEAR A CAPE AND TIGHTS.
(ALTHOUGH YOU CAN IF YOU WANT TO!)

Just make a difference.

Our world is in **desperate need** of strong leaders willing to **fight** for what they believe in.

You can do that—and you don't have to wait.
Just find something that you feel strongly about and

DO SOMETHING ABOUT IT.

If it bothers you that there are children
who don't have coats and sweaters for the winter,
ORGANIZE A CLOTHES DRIVE.

If the number of animals being put to sleep
keeps you up at night,
ORGANIZE AN ADOPTION DAY,
OR HELP EDUCATE PEOPLE ABOUT SPAYING AND NEUTERING.

If kids are being bullied or girls are harassed

in one area of your school, get a group of people together

AND TAKE TURNS HANGING OUT THERE

so nobody has to walk through that area by themselves.

get the idea?

All you need to do to be a hero is make positive changes.

And you can do that no matter how old you are
(or how you look in tights)!

There are BIG differences
between friends
and acquaintances.

ACQUAINTANCES are those we know and laugh and play with.
FRIENDS are those we love and laugh and cry with.

ACQUAINTANCES usually float in and out of your life,
but FRIENDS stick by you, through thick or thin.

ACQUAINTANCES sometimes develop into friends, but
never let a FRIEND drift into the role of acquaintance.

BOTH ARE NECESSARY AND BOTH ARE FUN.
Learn to tell the difference, and enjoy both.

There are thousands of people being paid lots of money
JUST TO SEPARATE YOU FROM YOURS!

Artists, musicians, and directors are all working together
to figure out how to make a product irresistible to you.

The more convincing they are at making you feel
you have to have a product—
THE MORE MONEY THEY MAKE.

If you look closely at what they are selling,
it is often not the product itself—
*it's beauty, popularity, self-confidence, or
other traits that can't be bought.*

If something out there could immediately and safely
MAKE YOU THIN, GET RID OF ACNE,
MAKE YOUR HAIR PERFECT EVERY DAY,
OR MAKE YOU IRRESISTIBLE TO OTHERS,

they wouldn't have to spend so much money to
convince you to buy it . . . **RIGHT?**

SEE ADVERTISING FOR WHAT IT IS.

When complimented, learn to just say "Thank you."

When you get a good grade or put together
an exceptionally great outfit and
know you look really good—**be glad other people notice!**

JUST SMILE AND SAY, "THANKS!"
AND RETURN THE COMPLIMENT IF YOU CAN.

Don't stand there and pretend that you didn't try to do or look good.
NOBODY WILL BELIEVE IT, AND IT JUST SOUNDS WEIRD.
Be proud of who you are, what you've done, and how you look.

If somebody notices and comments—

that's terrific.

If they don't—

well, YOU know; and that's enough!

Real life is BETTER than TV.

REAL LIFE
is not broken into neat hour-long segments.

Problems don't always end in time for commercial breaks.
There is no music to warn us
when something is about to happen.

If you know more about the characters on your favorite shows
than you do about your own family and friends—
YOU NEED TO GET OUT A LITTLE MORE.

Besides, how many hours of
perfect skin, elaborate hairdos,
and problems that are always miraculously solved in an hour
can you stomach?

THAT IS NOT REAL LIFE.

Life is more exciting and unpredictable than anything
that can be compressed into a show's time slot.

And best of all—NO commercial breaks!

The quickest way to start a conversation is to ask a question.

There is **one thing** that everyone is
comfortable and confident talking about—

themselves.

If you get stuck somewhere and
really want or need to talk to somebody—
find something to ask the person's opinion about . . .

clothing, music, whatever.

The best part about it is that it doesn't matter
who the person is or **what age** they are.

Whether you need to start a conversation with the president,
or that uncommunicative five-year-old you are baby-sitting,
everyone responds positively to a question about them.

That's the whole secret to getting a conversation off the ground—

now it is up to you to keep it going!

Don't get caught up in
trying to judge your own development or build your sense of worth
on where you perceive others to be.
There is really no way to do this and be fair to you.

Obstacles and events happen to people at different times.
OTHERS MAY LOOK LIKE THEY ARE HAVING A REALLY EASY TIME,
BUT MAY JUST BE AT A DIFFERENT POINT THAN YOU.

THEY MAY HAVE THE LESSONS THAT ARE MAKING IT TOUGH FOR YOU
BEHIND THEM, OR STILL IN FRONT OF THEM.

This is true even of your **own family members.**
It doesn't really matter if your sister or brother, or your mom or dad, was the
most popular, or the star athlete.

Those roles may be ones that you step into
or they may not ever be part of your life.

Live YOUR life at your own pace.

YOU CAN'T COMPARE YOURSELF TO OTHERS.

No one
has the right to
HURT,
BULLY, OR
INTIMIDATE
you.

GET AWAY OR GET HELP.

Most important, **tell** people **what is happening.**

If you try to tell someone and they don't listen or react,
TELL SOMEONE ELSE.

Bullies **lose their power** when you **lose your fear** of them.

They NEED you to feel afraid in order to be able to threaten you.

DON'T LET THEM USE YOUR FEAR AGAINST YOU.

There is safety in numbers—
let somebody know what is going on so you can't be cornered alone.

If someone has physically hurt you, or you feel like they truly will . . .

DO NOT DEAL WITH THIS ALONE.

GET HELP, AND GET IT FAST.

It doesn't matter who the threatening person is:
a classmate, a relative, a boyfriend, whoever—
they are doing something VERY wrong.

There is **nothing** that justifies someone being physically hurt.

YOU DO NOT DESERVE IT.

You need to get help from somewhere . . . quickly.

Really big decisions can't be second-guessed later on.

There comes a point with every choice, big or small,
WHERE YOU JUST HAVE TO MAKE IT.
You have as much information as you can get, and
you have to choose a path, right or wrong.

Choose it and then go on.

It will lead to other paths and people and experiences.

You can't really look back and figure out honestly
what would have happened if you had chosen differently.

You can guess where it may have led you,
but you'll never know for sure.

Had you made a different decision,
a completely different chain of events would have been set into motion.

The variations are dizzying to think about,
but as long as you keep heading in the right direction,
you'll get there (having gained
new information and experiences along the way).

You need to set aside time
for yourself.

Know what you are feeling
and understand the reasons why.

You have to study everything in order to learn about it—

THIS INCLUDES YOURSELF.

Getting to know yourself well takes a lot of
the guesswork
out of your decisions.

You don't have to figure out what everybody else is

THINKING OR DOING

to determine your reaction.

YOU CAN DO YOUR OWN THING—WITH CONFIDENCE!

Spend time learning about yourself.

WORDS CAN BE WEAPONS
AND THEIR WOUNDS TAKE A LONG TIME TO HEAL.

"Sticks and Stones may break my bones—but words can never hurt me."

THIS IS SO UNTRUE.
WORDS CAN REALLY, REALLY HURT.

Unlike scrapes and scratches that grow a scab to protect them, a wound left by unkind words stays tender for a long, long time.

CRUEL THINGS THAT WE SAY ARE WEAPONS;
AND THEIR BARBS LODGE DEEPER THAN WE REALIZE.

Most adults remember the hurtful things they were teased about.

With my dad it was his red hair. Mom told me how it hurt for people to tease that she disappeared if she turned sideways because she was so skinny.

The people who said these things so many years before probably don't even remember them—but the hurtful memories remain.

BE SO CAREFUL OF THE WORDS THAT SPRING FROM YOUR LIPS.
ONCE SAID, THERE REALLY IS NO WAY TO TAKE THEM BACK.

Become an expert on something.

WHAT INTERESTS YOU?

Horses?   Mysteries?

Dinosaurs?

Anime?   Films?

Music?   The Mayans?

Everyone should try to be **an expert** on something that fascinates them.

LEARN ALL YOU CAN ABOUT WHATEVER YOU LIKE.

It makes you both knowledgeable and interesting.

There are so many subjects that you HAVE to learn about, *isn't it great to choose one for yourself?*

You may find a way to turn what you enjoy into a career.

Being able to do something you REALLY LOVE as your profession is a rare thing—

but you can make it happen!

Everyone makes

BAD DECISIONS

sometimes.

So . . . when you dyed your hair RED you had more of a
Hollywood Diva thing in mind rather than the Little Orphan Annie
look you ended up with . . .

Or . . . that new friend who seemed so much older and cooler apparently has an
awful reputation that is now attached to you as well—even though you
haven't done anything . . .

Or . . . after trying and trying to get that impossibly cute guy to pay attention
to you—he has—and you've found out that
not only does he not have two brain cells to rub together,
he doesn't even seem as cute as he used to.

WHAT DO YOU DO?

Quick: Step back, rethink, and do something different!
It was just a bad decision; you can always make a different one.

Reputations can be overcome, and there are always other guys out there.
The hair thing requires a little more creativity—you may have to learn to love a
pixie cut for a while—but even that is temporary.

Just laugh or groan—
whatever it takes to feel better,

AND MOVE ON.

Your body's constant changes WILL settle down soon.

Why can't all of the parts of your body grow at the same rate?

The constant changes are not easy to deal with, but they are temporary.

EVERYTHING WILL BALANCE OUT IN TIME.

There's not a lot you can do other than to WAIT THEM OUT.

Your body has ITS OWN TIMETABLE for development.

Your body is and will be not only beautiful,

but uniquely yours.

When you do something great, speak up!
You earned it.

You know when you've done something really good—
from a project you went the extra mile on,
to a play you made in a game,
to just biting your tongue and letting someone else have space to talk
when you were dying to tell them something yourself.

When you've **worked hard** for something, you **deserve** praise,
particularly if you have done something that **wasn't easy.**

Be your own biggest fan.

The **older** you get, the **fewer** people around you will
OPENLY COMPLIMENT YOU.

Start training yourself now to **take pride**
in your own accomplishments.

There is nothing wrong with taking credit for the good you do.

Own your successes.

DON'T LET SOMEONE ELSE GOAD YOU INTO TROUBLE.

You won't really impress anyone.

We can all get ourselves into trouble
pretty easily without any outside help.

We don't need other people to suggest
new ways for us to mess up.

THOSE KIND OF OPPORTUNITIES LIE AROUND EVERY CORNER.

The next time somebody is trying
to talk you into something
you know is going to get you into trouble—

DON'T LET THEM.

***Your mistakes should be things to learn from,
not created for someone else's* ENTERTAINMENT.**

You now resemble
the person you will be in ten years
only as much as you now resemble
yourself a decade ago.

Step back ten years.

You couldn't do much
for yourself, or by yourself.

THINK ABOUT ALL YOU HAVE LEARNED IN THE PAST DECADE.

Ten years from now, you will have gone through as many changes
and hopefully picked up as much new information.

Every event adds to your knowledge.
Welcome all the new challenges and experiences.

**When you stop growing, you stop living—
and you have lots of growing, living, and learning to do!**

Let time teach you.

Love your Life

Every breath, every moment

–GOOD AND BAD–

is a precious gift.

REJOICE IN THE *good.*

LEARN FROM THE *bad.*

So many times we take the simple joy of
being alive for granted.

Just the fact that
we are here,
can make our own decisions,
move about without pain,
and experience all the world has to offer

is simply amazing.

There are so many WONDERFUL THINGS out there.
Be sure to fully love and live the life you have.

Spend every day as if tomorrow might not come,
and you will have NO REGRETS.

*Remember: Life is not a set amount of time—
it is a continuing journey.*

None of us knows how long we will be here—

Embrace it all.

**Friends hold us up when we are sinking,
laugh with us when we are happy,
and help us fully live and love the life we have.**

Think of the things you love people to do for you:

Remember your birthday   Call just to chat   Stand up for you
Know what you like and what you don't
Just listen when you need to talk   Make you feel special
Accept you as you are

DO THE SAME KINDS OF THINGS FOR YOUR FRIENDS.

Your friends don't have to
look like you, like the same things, or be the same age.

Friendship surpasses all of that. Some of my best friends have been
very different from me, and many of them have been guys.

*The superficial stuff **doesn't matter** as long as you can
really talk, listen, and have fun together.*

Treasure all your friends as the **precious gifts** they are, and
BE THE KIND OF FRIEND YOU DREAM OF HAVING.

CLOTHES THAT MAKE A STATEMENT
SHOULD SAY SOMETHING YOU BELIEVE.

The name of a band or a company or any other recognizable logo is
AN ADVERTISEMENT.

When you wear it,
you are advertising whatever they stand for.

IF YOU DON'T KNOW WHAT THEY STAND FOR, **FIND OUT.**

Groups that convince you to show off their brand names
are making you pay to advertise their products.

IT'S ALL ABOUT THEM MAKING MONEY.

You can still wear their clothes,
but wear them because they make you look good—

NOT because someone says you should.

Feel blessed—be thankful.

You have:
enough food to eat
    clothes to wear
        access to modern medical care
            and somewhere to go home to.

Not everyone has
a roof over their head, or education available to them.

Just knowing that the **food** we eat and the **water** we drink is clean
IS A CERTAINTY OTHER NATIONS WOULD LOVE TO HAVE.

There are people in our world right now, some in our own nation,
suffering daily from hunger, disease, poverty, and homelessness.

You have so much to be grateful for.

You are truly blessed.

Knowing this is one of the first steps toward
TRUE HAPPINESS AND CONTENTMENT.

Don't be afraid to live and learn
from your life right now.

You will gain knowledge that will serve you well as you grow older.

You can't **stop time** from passing,
and probably wouldn't want to if you could.

Each new phase of life brings with it
new joys, responsibilities, and things to explore.

DON'T FEAR GROWING UP.
Celebrate how far you've come and how much you have learned.

You have a WONDERFUL life ahead of you—
live it to the fullest, and

get inspired.

**Study great works of art, literature, and music.
There's something out there for everyone.**

MUSIC runs the gamut—
classical to jazz, scat to swing, the blues to experimental.
Sample as many types as you can.

SHAKESPEARE performed well can seize your heart
(we won't talk about it done badly!)
and PLATO'S SYMPOSIUM—debating the **true** nature of love—
is guaranteed to make you THINK.

Or just flip through a **glossy art book** and find what YOU like.

Some prefer *Degas' dancers*, others the twining strokes
of *van Gogh* or *Gauguin's tropical colors and people.*

AND EVERY CHANCE YOU GET,
GO AND SEE THE ORIGINALS.

I wandered into an exhibit of Rodin's sculpture with a friend one day,
and it took my breath away.

The artist had ripped handfuls of clay
from many of his perfect pieces before casting
so that the tearing was forever preserved in the bronze.

Rodin became real to me that day.
and THAT is the key.

Find what is REAL to YOU—

look at it—   hear it—
read it—   feel it—   experience it—

And then . . . create your own!

Believe GOOD THINGS
will happen to YOU.

Our beliefs become self-fulfilling prophecies.

If you are **convinced** that only **bad things** will happen,
you will focus on the events that support this belief.

If you **truly believe** that **good things** will come to you,
that is what you will perpetuate.

People will always live up to expectations placed on them—
HIGH OR LOW.

If you begin anything convinced that you cannot do it,
you probably will not be able to.

**People who believe good things will happen,
those who consider themselves "LUCKY,"
tend to have more good things happen to them.**

They see the bad as exceptions to the norm
and dwell on the good.
So get out there and look for the GOOD stuff,

you lucky girl!

DECIDE THE DIRECTION YOUR LIFE WILL TAKE.

Chart a course,
or set a goal for yourself.
Don't let yourself just be carried along.

YOU HAVE TO HAVE A PLAN TO GET ANYWHERE.

Every small detail doesn't have to be planned out,
but do have some idea of where you are going.

You will find that
many different paths can lead to the same destination.
As long as you keep heading in the right direction
you can explore different routes to get there.

In the journey of life,
knowing where you are headed is the important thing.

And as long as you stay focused,
YOU'LL GET THERE.

KNOW WHAT IS HAPPENING IN OUR WORLD.

**Stay up to date,
have your own opinions,
and never rely on just one source to back them up.**

Your generation will be the leaders of
our nation, businesses, and communities
sooner than you think.

There is A LOT OF INFORMATION and MANY STRONG OPINIONS on big issues.

You need to explore both sides
before deciding what YOU think.

People may disagree with you.
You may decide to change your mind as you gather more information.

But it certainly makes for interesting, lively discussions!

THIS STUFF IS IMPORTANT.
BE INFORMED.

People notice what you say and do.

There is very little we do that is not seen by someone.
This can be good.

Someone may see you doing some small, unexpected kindness
and it may challenge them to do something nice as well.

Or . . . you may say something ugly about someone
WITHOUT REALIZING SOMEONE HAS OVERHEARD YOU.

You have just changed the way that person sees you.
The fact that you said or did it when you thought no one was looking
just makes it worse.

Do you know someone who always has something
bad to say about other people?

Do you ever wonder what they say
to others about you when you aren't around?

Maybe you should. . . .

Follow your calling.

Maybe **your parents** are *lawyers*,
or **dentists**, or **farmers**,
or *whatever it is* **they chose to do.**

And maybe **their parents** had **the same occupation,**
as did **their parents,**

and so on.

OR MAYBE NO ONE IN YOUR FAMILY HAS EVER GONE TO COLLEGE,
AND THE ASSUMPTION IS THAT YOU WON'T EITHER.

Does this mean that you are required to follow suit?

ABSOLUTELY NOT!

What your parents, their parents, and other adults did or do
is the result of decisions they made.

Only you can decide what you want to
do with your life.

Play, dance, and laugh as often as you can.

We should always actively seek out playtime.
It is good for the soul.

Why not be silly if you have the chance?

Does it make you any less intelligent to play?
Of course not!

People who are fun and funny are people others LIKE TO BE AROUND.

Sometimes you will have to be serious,
but being mature and being serious are not the same thing.

MATURITY is knowing when to play around and when not to—
not forcing yourself to stop having fun all together.

A lack of play in your life just makes you feel

OLD AND TIRED—
(regardless of your age).

Situations can get STRANGE or HURTFUL.
        You get MIXED UP—
                CONFUSED—
                        you try to keep EVERYTHING INSIDE.

Everybody expects you to have it all together.

You worry about admitting you don't know what to do,
and you really just don't want to talk about it.

BUT YOU NEED TO.
YOU CAN'T DEAL WITH EVERYTHING YOURSELF.

Always keep somebody close you feel safe enough to talk to.
And give people a chance to listen and understand.

Just the act of talking something out can put it into perspective for you.
Things may not seem as scary or difficult once you say them aloud.

EVERY LOAD IS LIGHTER ONCE YOU SHARE THE WEIGHT, SO . . .

keep talking.

Tell someone if they make your day—

then pass it on!

It is so great when somebody does something wonderful
UNEXPECTEDLY.

No matter what kind of day you are having,
it suddenly becomes a whole lot better.

When this happens, stop and thank them—
then PASS THE GOOD FEELING ON to someone else.

Find an opportunity to make somebody's day,
and do it
(preferably at a completely unexpected moment).

It feels so good to make someone else happy.
The look of surprise on their face is so worth it!

EVERYONE NEEDS A PLACE TO CALL THEIR OWN.

*A place to go when you need
to be solitary,   to think,   to write,
or to just sit and relax.*

Find a spot where you won't be disturbed,
and let others know that when you are there
IT IS YOUR TIME.

*The spot may be
your bedroom, a comfy chair in the corner of a room,
a secluded place in the woods, the library,
or just a calming mental space you create.*

Retreat to it whenever you need to
REST, RECHARGE, OR JUST FIND SOME PEACE AND QUIET.

CLAIM SOME SMALL SPACE FOR YOURSELF.

Seek out people with talents different from yours.

Venture into an area different from your own talents.

Maybe you are really arty, but your best friend is into sports.
Sharing interests may expose you both to things you love,
AND WOULDN'T HAVE EXPLORED ON YOUR OWN.

OR find people whose talents *complement* yours.

If you are an incredible lead singer, you'll never put together
a great band by just looking for other singers.
You need people who can play the bass, the guitar,
the drums, and sing backup.

If you are a great artist, find someone who is an incredible author
AND PUT TOGETHER A BOOK.

There is no competition
when everybody has their own area of expertise.

You will ALL improve when you work together.

BUILD A STRONG SUPPORT SYSTEM.

It can be family, friends, the church—whatever works for you.

We all need people around who truly love us
when things get tough.

**And times will sometimes get tough;
that is the way life is.**

There is an oft-quoted example that compares a person's
strength to a stick. One stick alone can be snapped in half
with very little effort, but if you bundle many sticks together
they become more difficult, if not impossible, to break.

Your support system works the same way.

HARD TIMES CAN BREAK YOU IF YOU REMAIN BY YOURSELF.
But if you BIND WITH THE STRENGTH of others,
it takes much more force to tear through,

IF IT CAN BE DONE AT ALL.

Don't expect anyone to know what you need UNTIL YOU TELL THEM.

It is so easy to get angry
because your parents or other adults don't "get you"
or understand what is going on.

But unless you've told them, they don't know.

When was the last time you let them know
what was going on in your world?

It has probably been a while.

You are right,
the world adults live in **IS** very different from yours.
Until you explain the people and the situations you deal with,
they have to guess.

And their guesses will be based on their own past experiences,
which you know are outdated!

You can save a lot of frustration and time spent arguing
by simply explaining what life is like for you.

Our worlds are different.

Never let any boy make you think you are

UGLY, STUPID, OR NOT GOOD ENOUGH.

Girls mature more quickly. This INTIMIDATES some boys
and makes them ACT MEAN.

THEY MAY TRY TO MAKE YOU DOUBT OR FEEL BAD ABOUT YOURSELF.

Don't let it affect you.
Their world is tough, too.

Unfortunately, many boys feel like they have to
ACT TOUGH AND BE MEAN
to try to prove that they aren't as
worried, scared, or affected by stuff as everybody else.

Usually the bad behavior is just a sign of immaturity,
but in some it may be something they keep throughout life.

CHOOSE CAREFULLY WHOM YOU SPEND YOUR TIME WITH, AND
DON'T LET IMMATURE WORDS OR ATTACKS GET YOU DOWN.

Keep your body moving—
you'll feel and look great!

DO FUN THINGS—

turn up the music and dance,

climb a tree,

go skating,

turn cartwheels,

play tag with a little kid—

IT ALL COUNTS!

You have to keep moving to look and feel your best.

But there is no reason to think exercise has to be
something that is not fun—

you just have to be creative!

Your friends will be your GREATEST joys.

The ability to make, hold on to, and treasure our friends
is a wonderful gift.

The people you are exposed to in life are
there for a reason. Be thankful that you have had
the opportunity to spend time with those
you are blessed enough to call "FRIENDS."

Work to KEEP THE ONES YOU HAVE without ever shutting the door on
someone new. With luck, you can grow and change,
laugh and cry, and stand strong beside one another.

Throughout her life, my mother remained

BEST FRIENDS

with two girls she met in elementary school.

Despite many moves, job changes, miles, and years,
those three STUCK TOGETHER and STAYED IN TOUCH.

It was a beautiful thing to watch,
and a wonderful example to have set for me.

Now I keep up with Mom's friends
and I love to look through decades' worth of pictures of them
together—

ALWAYS LAUGHING, ARMS AROUND
ONE ANOTHER, JUST SO HAPPY TO
BE TOGETHER.

I can only hope to have friendships in
my life that measure up to theirs.

ENVY AND JEALOUSY
are not productive emotions.

You can't know what someone else's life is really like.
Every life is a mixture of good and bad.
No one has it easy all the time.
No amount of stuff can make you happy.
There will always be people with more than you,
and there will always be many more with less.

Being envious or jealous won't get you anything any quicker.

What these feelings will do is DESTROY contentment—
ONE OF THE NECESSARY INGREDIENTS FOR HAPPINESS.

If somebody has something you really want,
SHIFT YOUR THINKING.

See it as something you don't have YET—
instead of something you can't have.

Then use your energy to EARN it for yourself.

If you want people to RESPECT and LISTEN to you,
do the same for them.

There is **nothing** more frustrating
than trying to tell someone something and have them **not listen**
because they think they already have the answer
or they won't stop talking.

This is just as frustrating for other people.
Give them room to *express themselves,*
even if you don't agree with them.

Great conversations many times begin
with a difference of opinion.

Just keep your head and hold your ground.

Who knows? You may learn something *new!*

If you feel nervous and shy,
find somebody to talk to.

Nothing is as intimidating when there are two of you.
THERE IS SAFETY IN NUMBERS!

WHEREVER YOU ARE—
a new school,
a dance,
joining a club or team,
or trying out for a part in a play.
FIND SOMEBODY TO TALK TO.

If you are in the same place, you already have something in common.
Look around, find someone who looks approachable, and say "Hi."
Things are more fun if you have somebody to share them with.

So, make the first move!
A new friend may be standing right beside you.

Change is inevitable.

Don't try to stop it. Make it work for you instead.

While others stand still, wailing about how things aren't fair,
or get knocked off course by every wave of change,
STAND STRONG. You know the secret:

Change is always coming!

Acorns we can hold in the palm of our hands
become the towering oaks of tomorrow—
BUT ONLY IF THEY DON'T REMAIN ACORNS.

*Stretch your arms toward the sky, welcome the knowledge,
the growth, and the change necessary for you*

TO BECOME EVERYTHING YOU ARE MEANT TO BE.

EVERYONE IS BORN WITH UNIQUE, INNATE TALENTS.

Some can write, some can draw,
some lead others easily, some are very good at math.

Whatever you have, this is your STARTING POINT.
Work to DEVELOP the talent you have been granted.
It is your wonderful gift.

You may DEVELOP your talent into a career,
change the world (or at least your small corner of it!),
or ignore it and leave it lying on the ground—
a gaily wrapped present discarded and unused.

IT'S YOUR CHOICE.

But before you set your talent aside,
REMEMBER:
*Doing something you love—especially if you have a gift for it—
is a sure way to GUARANTEE success!*

DEVELOP YOUR NATURAL TALENT.

Everybody makes mistakes.

No one is perfect.

Mistakes can teach you things you wouldn't learn otherwise.
It is very **freeing** to be able to admit you **really messed up**
this time . . .
and know the truth of your words.

People who refuse to admit they make mistakes can't empathize when others
mess up. Or they feel the need to go into a long explanation of what YOU
should have done differently.

You don't need to hear that.
And no one else does either, from you or anybody else.

By giving yourself the FREEDOM to make mistakes,
you learn to accept when OTHERS do the same thing.

And that makes even BIG blunders worth something!

BECOME SELF-SUFFICIENT.

*Y*ou don't have to worry about paying the bills,
or putting food on the table.
But do the small stuff.

Wash your own clothes,
clean up your room when it needs it,
load the dishwasher,
take care of your pets.

Just start taking care of yourself.
If you want to be TREATED like you are more grown-up,
HANDLE YOUR OWN RESPONSIBILITIES.

Consider it training for later.

Pretend your room is your own apartment,
and keep it *nice,*
JUST FOR YOU.

Talk about your dreams and goals.

The more people you tell about your dreams and goals—
the more information you will receive.

You will get more good leads from a casual mention of
something than you will believe!

I had painted and sculpted for years, but had never shown my work. Then I told a
few people about it, and they mentioned it to others, and I found out about local
artists groups and other opportunities to meet others like myself.

*Doors to **new friends and experiences** opened up that I never
could have found on my own.*

Help often comes from the most UNLIKELY places.

Life confuses everyone sometimes.

No one has all the answers, because every situation is unique.

Even adults who seem to have it all together get
OVERWHELMED and CONFUSED.
WE ARE ALL JUST DOING THE BEST WE CAN.

I remember being SO intimidated in school because other people
seemed to have it all together—
they knew what to say, when to say it, what to wear to every event.

I thought I was the only one who was making it up as I went along.

Years later I talked to some of those "PULLED TOGETHER" people,
and I found out that everybody, even they, had been just feeling their way along!
They had been as much in the dark as I was.

Even those who seemed to look and function perfectly with no
hesitation suffered from bouts of SELF-DOUBT—just like me!

I wish someone had told me that while I was living through it.
Things would have been so much easier.

THERE IS NOTHING YOU CANNOT OVERCOME.
*You are strong and capable enough to overcome
anything life throws at you.*

And life will probably give you many chances to prove this.
Recognize your individual strengths—
before you have reason to need them.

**Some things take longer than others to beat,
but with perseverance you will prevail.
Self-doubt will try to knock you off balance,
but don't let it—or get right back up after it does.**

Working through tough times makes similar experiences
much easier to get through.

*Think of life as a game. You have certain strengths and people to
work with. The GOAL is to use them in the right order or
combination, so you move on to the next level.*

Many times it takes several tries to get it right.
BUT KEEP WORKING AT IT—AND YOU'LL WIN.

What seems like A LOT OF MONEY to you now will look COMPLETELY DIFFERENT later on.

Remember this when your after-school job starts looking like a career.

What happens when you

start a family
or want to buy a house
or get a chance to travel?

You can live with less or more—you decide.

Years spent in school to make a good living may seem eternal.
But if you don't, the years you spend working harder than everybody else for less money will seem much longer.

Education and hard work are the only way to secure your financial future.

THERE ARE NO SHORTCUTS.

Be patient.
Be willing to invest time and effort toward your goal.

Instant gratification is always a trap.

Volunteer your time and talent as often as you can.

Your **talent** is something special that you have been given,
and you should **share it**.

There is SOMETHING SPECIAL about giving away your time or talent freely.
You get a warm feeling of both DOING AND BEING GOOD.

Willingly giving of yourself opens you up to do and feel more.

You will learn that it is not only the people you are helping who
benefit, you will also. You gain *knowledge, contentment,* and a
feeling of self-worth that comes only from helping other people.

So many people out there could benefit from the knowledge, talent,
or simply the extra time that you have.

Share what you have been given with others,
and maybe someday when you are in need,
someone will do the same for you.

NEVER DOUBT YOUR STRENGTH.

We are not handed anything in life that we cannot handle.

Things may seem insurmountable,
but you will find a way through or around every obstacle.

And you will be stronger and smarter for having overcome.

When faced with a situation that looks too big to deal with, SHIFT YOUR FOCUS. Look at it from a different angle.

Your eventual victory may be the only way for you to prove how strong you really are. Above all, DON'T GIVE UP.

If life is constantly pounding you, take pride in the fact that your trials are proof of your strength.

A weaker person possibly couldn't handle your life—

BUT YOU CAN, AND YOU WILL.

Know Yourself.

Don't rely on other people's opinions to determine who you are or how you are doing.

Trying to base your self-worth on how others view you is like trying to see what you look like in a funhouse mirror. What you see reflected back will bend, twist, and change, depending on the other person's mood and what is going on in their life.

No one wants the responsibility of being in charge of your entertainment or emotional well-being—
THEY HAVE THEIR OWN THINGS TO DEAL WITH.

This sets both of you up for constant frustration.

It is important to **spend time alone**. It may feel uncomfortable at first, but your **discomfort level** is equal to how dependent you have become on other people's input. With practice you will learn to **trust your own instincts** and be

comfortable in your OWN skin.

Nothing you can put on can give you the same glow as being healthy and happy.

And if you have a natural glow of good health and contentment, you can wear anything and look good!

It works both ways.

What you have right now, without doing anything, is what every cosmetic company in the world is trying desperately to sell—YOUTH.

WOMEN SPEND A FORTUNE ON PRODUCTS THAT PROMISE TO GIVE THEM THE GLOW OF YOUTH.

You've got it for free!

Enjoy it and play it up.
You don't have to try to look older or use lots of products—
just stay healthy, be happy, and you will shine.

YOU CAN ALWAYS WALK AWAY FROM VERBAL ATTACKS.

**Angry, mean people usually feel miserable.
You don't have to participate in their misery.**

They gain power when you lose your stability or emotional footing. So they'll try to make you lose your temper, react in the heat of the moment, or not think through your reactions.

**Distance—emotional, physical, or both—will help you.
Don't let the barbs being slung at you stick.
Imagine them just bouncing off.**

*Take a long, slow breath—
Regain your balance—
Respond calmly—
Or just walk away.*

When somebody singles you out for attack, they are looking for a reaction. If they can't get one from you, they will look elsewhere. Don't give them what they want. Fight the urge to lower yourself to their level.

And **N E V E R** let them know they got to you—
or they will be **BACK FOR MORE.**

Make positive changes in your world.

Start small.

PICK UP THE TRASH THAT IS ON YOUR STREET, IN FRONT OF YOUR HOUSE, OR AROUND YOUR SCHOOL.

Write a letter every month or so to your grandparents telling them what's going on in your life.

Volunteer to walk an elderly person's dog or help with something else they can't do easily.

SET THE TABLE.

Call somebody you haven't talked to in a while— just to say hello.

DO YOUR HOMEWORK WITHOUT BEING ASKED.

Read a book to a little kid.

When your parents ask how your day was—tell them—and then ask them about theirs.

If you want your corner of the world to be a better, nicer place, it has to start with *you*.

Do your part, and hope that others follow your example.

BE CONFIDENT AND PROUD.

Most of us can list our faults more readily than the good things about us.

Why is that?

It doesn't do you any good to carry around a mental list of everything that is wrong with you.

GET RID OF IT.

Focus on the things that make you GREAT.
HOLD YOUR HEAD HIGH and revel in all the GOOD THINGS about you.

I know an incredible woman who has succeeded in many areas that other people only dream about without any formal training.

I asked her once what the secret was:
How can she just DO the things others are AFRAID TO TRY?

She said she does get intimidated sometimes.
Then she looks at the people she is competing with and
tells herself that although they may have
more experience,   more money,   or be better looking,
she is S M A R T E R than they are.

And because she is smarter, she is going to win . . . and she does.

A perfect example of sheer self-confidence put into action—
with enviable results!

Enjoy being a girl for as long as you can.

**You don't have to be in such a rush to
be or seem older than you are.**

**You'll have years to spend being an adult,
but you only get to be this age once—**

Try out different looks, act goofy,
and experiment to see what you like.

Right now you have the freedom to just be YOU.

So laugh and play and dance and goof around with your friends.

And if some VERY SERIOUS PERSON looks down their nose at you
and tells you to "GROW UP,"

tell them you will—when it's time!

OTHER PEOPLE'S OPINIONS CAN'T AFFECT YOU UNLESS YOU LET THEM.

When someone says something NEGATIVE about you
or something you feel strongly about,

consider the source:
Take into account who is saying it.

If it is someone who knows you well or someone who truly has your best interests at heart, the opinion may warrant further consideration. But if it is someone you don't know or who knows little if anything about you—take it as an uninformed opinion.

It may have merit; it may not—
either way, it is still just one person's opinion.

AND IT'S COMING FROM SOMEONE WHO DOESN'T EVEN KNOW YOU.

First loves rarely last forever.

They fall victim to time, change, growth, or distance.
And the crushing pain of a first love ending is
something we don't forget.

It feels like you will never be able to
let yourself love someone again.

But you are worthy of love.

NOT BECAUSE SOMEONE LOVES YOU,
but because you HAVE THE ABILITY to love.

And as long as you don't shut yourself off, love will find you.

Don't become like Sleeping Beauty and hide your heart
and yourself behind a thick, impenetrable wall of thorns
because you've been hurt. Have the courage to cut the
thorns yourself, and be brave enough to reveal your true
self, faults and all, to those who WANT TO GET CLOSE TO YOU.

RELATIONSHIPS THAT FAIL DON'T MATTER IN THE LONG RUN—
ONLY THE ONES THAT SUCCEED.

ACT THE SAME WHEN YOU ARE ALONE
AS YOU DO AROUND OTHER PEOPLE.

My grandmother used to say,
"CHEATING IS CHEATING."

Meaning even if you made a "minor adjustment"
to the cards in a game of solitaire, you still cheated,
whether anybody saw you do it or not.

People's true selves emerge
when they think no one can see them.

If you want to know what someone is *really like*—
watch carefully what they do when *they think they are alone.*

AND REALIZE SOMEONE MAY BE DOING THE SAME TO YOU!

LEARN BASIC SELF-DEFENSE.

Think about animal predators, like lions.
How do they choose which animal in a herd to attack?
They always choose the one who looks the WEAKEST.

THERE IS SOMETHING TO BE LEARNED FROM THAT FACT.

Predatory people:
a bully in your school,
somebody with a chip on their shoulder,
or someone much more dangerous,
will do the same thing.

They look for weakness and single out victims
who don't look like they can take care of themselves.
That's where SELF-DEFENSE comes in.

You may never need to use it, but knowing
you could defend yourself gives you a different "vibe."
You carry yourself more confidently.

Besides, MARTIAL ARTS or KICKBOXING or
whatever you choose
is great exercise.

LOOKING GOOD IS AN ADDED BENEFIT!

Pressure to make a **QUICK DECISION** is a warning to give it
PLENTY OF THOUGHT.

*There is no decision you need to make that you can't take a little
time to think about. The more important the decision, the more time
you need to spend on it.*

*When someone else wants you to decide a certain way,
they will try a couple of things:*
**Information will be presented so it looks as though
there is only ONE LOGICAL SOLUTION, or you'll be pressured to
MAKE UP YOUR MIND very quickly.**

BOTH OF THESE STRATEGIES SHOULD SEND UP RED FLAGS.

Take the pressure as a warning, and look CAREFULLY before you commit. Don't be
afraid to say you need time to think about it.

**Be comfortable with your decisions,
and know WHY you made the ones you did.**

Do things that make you proud of yourself.
The basics you need to succeed—

self-confidence, strength, fearlessness,
determination, joy, and contentment—

come from taking pride in
WHO YOU ARE and WHAT YOU DO.

**Gird yourself with the knowledge of as many of your
positive attributes as you can. They SHIELD YOU from
BAD THINGS that happen and help to BUFFER LIFE'S BLOWS.**

Pride in yourself is a very powerful weapon. It reminds you
that you are worth a lot and can list the reasons why,
even if someone is trying to tell you differently.

*Doing things that make you proud are worth doing for that reason
alone. Stay familiar with all the good things you do—
making somebody happy, going the extra mile on a project,
standing up for yourself or a friend—and revel in them.*

Even if nobody else notices, you know,

and THAT IS ENOUGH.

State your opinions and ideas confidently.

If you have a point to make or an opinion to state—JUST SAY IT.

And say it with confidence. Look the person in the eye and make your point. The more important what you have to say is, the greater the need to state yourself clearly.

You can't expect anyone to take you seriously if you are mumbling at the floor or sound like you are apologizing. You DON'T HAVE TO BE APOLOGETIC for having an opinion or an idea.

Everyone is entitled to an opinion—

claim yours,

state it clearly,

then wait to see what happens.

It is better to have a few nice things than a lot of cheap stuff.
QUALITY BEFORE QUANTITY!

If you only buy cheap things, you will have to replace them a lot more often, and it will cost you more over time.

Just buy QUALITY and take care of it.

Here's a simple secret—

Divide the price of something by the number of times you will use it. That gives you some idea of how much you are really spending. Use your clothes as an example. Things that you will wear a lot—a wardrobe's "building blocks"— should cost more than something cool but really trendy that you will only wear for a season.

Spend more on what you use the most.

BUY THE fun stuff, TOO, BUT
DON'T LET IT BREAK THE BANK.

Sometimes you outgrow friendships.
It is sad, but it happens.

*There are times when a friend may choose a path
that you don't feel comfortable following—
and you begin to grow apart.*

*Or you may move or go to different
schools or just start hanging out
with different groups of people.*

THINGS HAPPEN THAT WE CAN'T FORESEE.

**Friendships are not just BLACK AND WHITE—there are a
lot of gray areas. Try to SPREAD YOUR NET WIDE and
have lots of different people as friends.**

THAT WAY, IF YOU DO GROW AWAY FROM ONE PERSON OR
GROUP, YOU WILL HAVE OTHERS TO HELP BRIDGE THE GAP.

DON'T STAND BY WHEN SOMETHING YOU DON'T AGREE WITH IS GOING ON.

If you stand and watch while someone is being ATTACKED, you are as guilty as the person doing the damage.

There is strength in numbers, and if you stand there while someone does something rotten, you are supporting them by being there and not objecting.

Be brave enough to say something or just walk away.

We've all seen a bully attack while a bunch of people just stand around. Do you think the bully would be as brave if everyone watching moved to stand beside and support the person being attacked, leaving the bully all alone?

There is a very true phrase, "GUILT BY ASSOCIATION," which is worth remembering when you are being pulled into a BAD SITUATION—even as a spectator.

Sometimes you have to look into your *future* to get through *today*.

LONG-TERM GOALS CAN BE HARD TO STAY COMMITTED TO.

You have to remind yourself where you are going to stay on track.
Looking ahead can help with decisions, too.

If someone is trying to push you into doing
something you are unsure of—
think of what it may do to your future.
Will it give people reason to talk badly about you?
Nobody wants more of that kind of attention.
If someone wants you to let them cheat,
or take something from a store,
the long-term consequences could be severe.

Train yourself to look beyond the here and now.

Most actions have some type of lasting impact.

If you can see what the impact could be,
your decisions become much easier.

DON'T BEAT YOURSELF UP OVER PAST MISTAKES.

You are in a transition period. You are going to have to be **brave enough** to give this growing stage the **best shot** you can and NOT WORRY SO MUCH ABOUT MESSING UP.

No one does anything perfectly the first time they try it. So give yourself a break.

If you do something and aren't happy with the way it worked out, try something different next time. These trials and errors are necessary for you to figure out who you are and what you want to do.

It's OK. Whatever happened—good or bad—it's over.

Tomorrow is another day, and in ten years no one will even remember it.

Sometimes the BEST THING you can do for someone is just listen.

Many times the ONLY THING you can do for someone is just listen.

**There is so much confusing stuff going on that
sometimes you just have to talk it out.**

YOU DON'T REALLY NEED INPUT—YOU JUST WANT TO TALK.

Thank goodness for those who have the rare gift of
being able to really listen.

*A receptive, nonjudgmental ear,
a hug,
"I'm so sorry that happened," or
"I understand"
have many times been my saving grace when I got
completely overwhelmed.*

Now I try to return the favor as often as I can!

IT TAKES TIME TO REALLY GET TO KNOW SOMEONE.

AN INSTANT ATTRACTION OR SHARED INTERESTS ARE BOTH GREAT PLACES TO START, BUT FOR FRIENDSHIPS AND RELATIONSHIPS TO GO THE DISTANCE, THEY HAVE TO STAND THE TEST OF TIME.

It is so easy, when a friendship or relationship is new,
to convince yourself that you and the other person
have everything in common.

Given time, we sometimes find that one of two things may have colored what looks to be a perfect pairing:

Either the other person
is attempting to be
whatever or whomever
we are looking for

or we are projecting ourselves
onto them—seeing all of our
likes and dislikes reflected
back from them.

In the beginning, both of these things can be incredibly convincing.

THERE IS NO DANGER IN LETTING TIME PROVE WHAT YOU FEEL YOU ALREADY KNOW. IF YOU HAVE TRULY FOUND A SOUL MATE, THAT IS MAGICAL AND WONDERFUL AND SOMETHING THAT WILL LAST. IF THE FACADE STARTS TO CRUMBLE, JUST BE PROUD OF THE FACT THAT YOU KNEW ENOUGH TO LET TIME JUDGE.

Laugh at your own mistakes.

Sometimes things get so bad, or you do something SO DUMB, it just gets funny. There are times when only laughing at the situation will help.

There is also no better way to DIFFUSE AN ATTACK than to make a joke about it. People CAN'T FIGHT with someone who is laughing along at whatever they just did.

If you can get past the immediate awfulness of whatever happened, you may realize it IS funny. Or it would be—if it had happened to anybody but you!

So TAKE A DEEP BREATH, roll your eyes, and laugh along with everyone else.

It really will be OK.

Be TRUSTWORTHY.

It is IMPOSSIBLE to have a real conversation with
someone you don't feel is trustworthy, and
IT'S TRULY IMPOSSIBLE TO BE FRIENDS WITH THEM.

**Trust is one of the basic building blocks of
friendship and personal contentment.**

So how do you build trust?

Take your word seriously.
Only promise things you can actually do.
Keep your friends' secrets.
Do the right thing when no one is watching.
Tell the truth . . . always.

TRUST CAN TAKE YEARS TO BUILD,
but only seconds to destroy.

Nobody "owes" you anything.

Not your parents,
not your friends,
certainly not the world at large.

You get things in life either because you WORK HARD to earn them or THROUGH SHEER HAPPENSTANCE.

There is no *universal list* that determines what each person should have for the world to be "FAIR."

Your life and the free will to do with it what you will is alone an indescribable gift.

We have been given *all that we need and more—*
TO FEEL WE ARE OWED MORE IS THANKLESS.

You deserve what you settle for.

This was one of my grandmother's favorite retorts to my frequent bouts of whining while I was growing up.

**I would complain about all sorts of things—
guys who didn't appreciate me,
dull and boring jobs that were beneath me,
my run-down apartment—**

And she would always say, "You deserve what you settle for."

And she was right.

My grumbling was usually the result of my own decisions. I would try to take the easiest route, to make the choice that required the least amount of work on my part. And then I would be DISAPPOINTED with the result.

AS I LEARNED NOT TO "SETTLE" FOR LESS THAN I REALLY WANTED, MY FRUSTRATION LEVEL—AND WHINING BINGES—DECREASED DRAMATICALLY.

CHOOSE WHETHER TO FOLLOW OR LEAD.

Our world needs followers as well as leaders.
Plans wouldn't go anywhere if people couldn't work together.

*If you want to be a leader, be prepared: Leading is not
doing what everyone else does, or getting everyone to like
you. Leadership requires much more from a person.*

GOOD LEADERS

are not driven by the need for personal recognition or prestige,

are fearless enough to take suggestions,

can separate personal needs from common goals,

know how to inspire a group,

are willing to let each individual do their part,

and take responsibility for the outcome.

If you are up to the challenge, LEAD ON!
If you AREN'T QUITE READY YET—that's fine, too.

Just be choosy about whom you follow and where.

Attitudes are contagagious.

**Do you know somebody who can make you laugh?
I mean, a real "hurt your sides and make you cry" kind of laugh?**

Lucky you!

Hang on to them.
And be that kind of person for somebody else.

They'll love you for it!

*A really happy person lifts you up a little just to be around
them. That's why people love to be around others who have a
great outlook and a good sense of humor.*

THERE IS A FLIP SIDE TO THIS. TERMINAL CASES OF **BAD ATTITUDE** OR
THE **GRUMBLES** ARE JUST AS CONTAGIOUS. WATCH OUT;
THEY CAN SUCK THE LIGHT OUT OF EVERY SITUATION AS EASILY AS
THE GOOD-NATURED CAN ADD IT.

Surround yourself with colors that make you HAPPY.

My daughter redecorated her room.
The walls are an incredibly deep, vibrant periwinkle, with a huge
painting of a crescent moon—all swirling lavenders,
purples, greens, and blues. It is calming and serene.
And the entire space is uniquely hers.

My sister's childhood room—
bright oranges and yellows—
a riot of color and shapes—
echoed her very vibrant personality.

YOUR COLORS ARE AS INDIVIDUAL AS YOU ARE.

Colors you love can help calm you, make you happy,
or feel more secure. I love black and green. Anytime I am
feeling nervous or unsure, I try to wear my favorite colors.

Experiment and see if using your colors works for you.

See the big picture.

*Life is a puzzle box filled to the brim with unconnected pieces,
a jumble of shapes and colors. Everyone has to assemble it,
by themselves and in their own time.*

Just to make it more of a challenge, there are lots of random, unrelated pieces
dumped in along with duplications. We don't know what belongs and what doesn't.
Then we see there may be a pattern or connections between individual pieces.
Every piece is a part of your life—an event, a person, or a path before you.

Some will start by focusing on just one color or shape—others build all the edges
first. There is no necessary order for success, only perseverance is required.

Sometimes we spend a lot of time trying to make **one piece** *fit.
It may never work. You didn't do anything wrong.*
THAT PIECE JUST DIDN'T BELONG IN YOUR BOX.

Some will finish quickly. Others will find it too frustrating and put the
whole box away so they don't have to look at it. Whether you stick
with it long enough to see the big picture is your choice—
but no one knows how long you have to work.

The more you work, the *clearer* and *easier* the connections are
to see. And if you are able to slip that last piece into place, the
result is a *beautiful* thing to behold.

Don't let stuff you have or want take over your life.

There are so many things that we want or feel like we NEED.
Knowing what you want and working toward it is a good thing.
Just don't let the "wanting" start taking over, because GETTING MORE
STUFF won't make you content.

There will always be someone who has more than you do.

IF YOU FIND YOURSELF
focusing on the things you want to the extent
that you can't enjoy what you have,

getting angry with others who seem to have more,

worrying constantly that somebody is going to take your stuff, or

trying to find any way—LEGAL OR OTHERWISE—to get the stuff
you want . . . there's a problem.

The things you have DO NOT define you.

Never give up
on something
that is truly important
to you.